A KID'S GUIDE TO THE POWER OF WORDS

TONY EVANS

HARVEST Kids™

HARVEST HOUSE PUBLISHERS
EUGENE, OREGON

A KID'S GUIDE TO THE POWER OF WORDS

Copyright © 2018 by Tony Evans
Published by Harvest House Publishers
Eugene, Oregon 97408
www.harvesthousepublishers.com

ISBN 978-0-7369-7298-7 (pbk.)
ISBN 978-0-7369-7340-3 (eBook)

Printed in the United States of America

18 19 20 21 22 23 24 25 26 / BP-CD / 10 9 8 7 6 5 4 3 2 1

Contents

Say What?

Imagine a world without words. You couldn't talk to people. You couldn't text people. You couldn't read or write anything. Nobody would have a name. In fact, *nothing* would have a name. Nobody could read directions, like how to bake a cake or how to get somewhere. You couldn't read a book or watch a movie with characters that talk to each other. Songs would have no words. Just look around and listen. How many words do you see? How many words do you hear?

Words have a lot of power in our world! And *your* words have a lot of power as well. You can use your words to make new friends. You can use your words to help your brother or sister when they're sad or frustrated. You can use your words to encourage someone on your sports team or in your dance class. And you can use your words to share the love of Jesus with everyone around you.

The words you speak are important, and so are the words you text or leave as comments on social media. Even the words you *think* are important. You may never say what you're thinking out loud or write down your thoughts for anyone else to read, but those words still affect someone—they affect *you*.

In this book, I'm going to use words to talk about the power of words. And you'll be able to write down words of your own to help you learn and grow and discover how to use your words in the best way possible.

You can use your words to praise God and draw closer to Him. You can use them to develop wisdom and maturity. You can use your words to bless and build up other people. You can use them to show God and others how thankful you are for all they've done for you. And you can use your words to help the people you care about.

If you're having trouble with your words, don't give up. Our words reflect what's in our hearts, and we need to work on the heart first. When your heart is in the right place, your words will show that. When Jesus is in your heart, Jesus is in your words.

Words have power. And *the* Word—the Bible, the Word of God—has the most power of all. If you're ever unsure of what to say in a difficult situation, God's got your back. He is more than happy to help you make His words your words. And when you allow God to help you with your words...well, get ready for some amazing stuff to happen!

We can make a difference with our words. We can influence people with our words. We can change the world with our words.

Are you ready? Grab a pen (because each chapter has fun fill-in-the-blank activities to get your brain going) and a highlighter (if you like to mark stuff that way) and maybe even a notebook so you can jot down your favorite verses and ideas. We're going to tap in to some serious power—the power of your words!

Words Are Powerful

ave you ever played Jenga? Players build a tower of blocks and then take turns removing one block each turn until the tower falls. When you first build the tower, it's super sturdy and seems like it would be impossible to knock over by pulling out just one block. But every time you remove a block, the tower weakens. And finally all you need to do is remove one more block to make the entire structure come crashing down.

Our words are like Jenga blocks. We can stack them up, block by block, into a strong and sturdy structure. We use good words to build the tower—positive words, encouraging words, true words. But then all it takes is one negative word to send the tower crashing to the ground.

All of us have our own set of Jenga blocks—the words we speak. We can use them for good or for evil—to build something strong or to tear something down. Our words are incredibly powerful, but most of us don't even realize we have this strength.

God created each one of us and gave us the power to construct or to demolish. And that power is in the tongue. When we speak words—to others, to God, and even to ourselves—we put that power to work.

Training the Tongue

Try talking without using your tongue. It's impossible, isn't it? You might be able to make some funny sounds, but nobody would understand your actual words. Your tongue might not seem very important, but it is. That three-inch muscle in your mouth has the power to make friends or to make enemies. It has the power to make people feel happy about themselves or to make them feel sad. And it has the power to speak truth or to speak lies. That's a lot of power for something about the size of a few Jenga blocks!

WATCH YOUR MOUTH!

If your mom is like mine, she probably tells you the same thing my mom used to tell me: "Watch your mouth!" I would say something I probably shouldn't have said, and my mom would march right over to me with a stern look and say, "Boy, you'd better watch your mouth!" Then, depending on what it was she'd heard me say, she might tell me to go wash my mouth out with soap!

Have you ever had to wash your mouth out with soap? It's disgusting—wiping that bar of soap on your tongue long enough to show your mom you actually did it. You feel like gagging. It's totally gross. I know I didn't have to wash my mouth out with soap twice—once was enough for me to learn that lesson!

I'm guessing nobody is going to wash your mouth out with soap today, but think about the words you've said recently. Have they been good words? Nice words? Positive words? Make sure the answer is yes because it's easier to keep your mouth clean than to wash it out.

Learning to control your tongue is important because the mouth has a ton of power. You might be playing a sport or excelling in an activity because someone once told you that you had natural talent or skill. Perhaps you're doing really well in a school subject because your teacher has given you a lot of encouragement and praise. Your friendships could be strong because you hang out with people who say positive things and build each other up. A lot of good can come from words that are positive, encouraging, and true.

On the other hand, words—even just a few words—have the power to affect you in a negative way. If somebody calls you "stupid" or "loser," your confidence can disappear pretty quickly. You start thinking that maybe you're not a very good singer or student or soccer player. You take the other person's negative words into your own mind and heart, and then you start saying them to yourself. And that's *really* damaging.

The Bible says some important things about the words that come out of our mouths. Colossians 4:6 says, "Let your conversation be always full of grace, seasoned with salt, so that you may know how to answer everyone." And if you don't prefer salt, how about honey? "Gracious words are a honeycomb, sweet to the soul and health to the bones" (Proverbs 16:24).

What are some words that give you confidence and make you feel good about yourself?

Beautiful   Helpful
Kind   Friendly
Smart

What are some words that make you feel sad or discouraged?

Stupid   Ugly
Smelly
Dirty (Buddy)

No Small Thing

Choosing which words to say is no small thing. Whether you are talking to a friend, a parent, a sibling, or a kid you met at the park, your words carry a ton of power. Just as removing one Jenga block can topple a tower, speaking one wrong word can mess up an entire situation. But don't worry—speaking the right word can go a long way to putting things back together.

You have the power to totally change up a situation with your words. If you're hanging out with a group at school and one kid starts making fun of someone else, you have three choices.

- You can choose not to say anything, which basically means you're going along with the mean kids.

- You can choose to add your own insults or put-downs and make the situation even worse.

- Or you can choose to use your words for good. You can say, "Hey, let's talk about something else." Or "That's my friend you're talking about."

Your words have power—and your good words have the greatest power of all.

The best place to go for good words is the Bible. That's where we can find out what God says about different situations, like getting along with others and helping people feel good about themselves. We should pay careful attention to those words because what comes out of God's heart is always right and true. That's why reading the Bible and memorizing verses are such terrific things to do. They give you instant access to the best kind of words—ones that come directly from God.

How can you use your words to make a positive difference in a hard situation?

_____

_____

_____

Say It, Do It

Did you know that if you can learn to control what you say, you can also control what you do? It's true. The words you speak can have a major effect on your actions.

Have you ever been in a situation where you didn't want to do something, but you talked yourself into it? Maybe you were trying to convince yourself to jump off the high dive for the first time. Or hop up onto the back of a horse. Or even get up the courage to introduce yourself to someone else. *Come on*, you might have told yourself. *You've got this!*

What are some words you can use to talk yourself into doing something or to pump yourself up?

_____

_____

_____

You can also talk yourself *out* of things. You want to join the track team, but you're afraid you're too slow and won't ever be able to run fast. You've kept hearing awesome things about your church's summer camp, but you're scared that when you get there, you won't want to stay overnight or you'll get too homesick. You want to get to know some of the kids in your class better, but you're worried that they will say no if you invite them over to your house.

Remember, when you're talking to yourself, that's also a good time to talk to God. Whether you're feeling excited or scared, happy or sad, confident or discouraged, God will always be there. And if you don't have any words of your own to use, you can go to the Bible and borrow some of God's words, like the ones in the book of Psalms. His words are there for you to use!

Look in the Bible (the book of Psalms is always a good place to start) and write down some words from God that will help you when you're needing words of help.

_____

_____

_____

BiT AND BRiDLE

When our kids were young, my wife and I took them to family camp each summer, and we usually got to spend some time riding horses. If you've ridden a horse before, you know that you can control a 1500-pound beast of an animal with a little piece of metal placed just right in its mouth. If I wanted to make the horse go left, all I needed to do was move the reins so that the bit in his mouth guided him in the direction I wanted to go. If I wanted to stop, I simply pulled back, and the bit in the horse's mouth brought him to a complete stop.

It's fun to ride a horse that goes where you want it to go, but I sure wouldn't want to get on the back of a wild stallion. There's no way I could control a horse like that. It would buck me right off.

The tongue is like a bit in a horse's mouth. It's a small muscle, but it can take control of your whole life. And if you let it lead you the wrong way, it can do some serious damage to you and to others. This especially happens when you're angry or frustrated and you spout out the first thing that pops into your head. So control that tongue! Use it to steer your life in the right direction.

Act Your Age (at Least!)

Probably one of the worst things someone can say about you is that you're *immature*. When someone calls you immature, they mean you act younger than your age and younger than other people your age. That's not a good thing!

Your words can show exactly how mature—or immature—you are. James 3:2 says, "We all stumble in many ways. If anyone does not stumble in what he says, he is a mature man who is also able to control his whole body."

We all make mistakes and say or do things we shouldn't, but our goal should always be to control ourselves. And that begins with controlling our tongues. If you can learn to control what you say, you'll also be able to control what you do.

A person who speaks kind words to others and doesn't talk back or put others down will be able to make friends. Someone who uses a lot of positive and encouraging words will be chosen as a team captain or a group leader. Kids who can laugh at themselves and remain cheerful are often the most well-liked. And if you're not sure what to say, just putting a smile on your face can change things for the better.

A mature person looks for the good in other people and situations—and their words show this.

A lot of Christians place a high value on going to church, being in a Bible study, praying before meals, and other actions. Those things are super important, but the one way to know you are a mature Christian is by noticing what comes out of your mouth. The Bible says, "If anyone thinks he is religious without controlling his tongue, then his religion is useless and he deceives himself" (James 1:26).

So watch your words!

What are some things mature Christians might say when they hear someone using their words to bully someone else?

_____

_____

_____

What are some words you can use to show that you look for the good in a person or in a situation?

_____

_____

_____

Just a Spark

Did you know that a huge forest fire can be started with just a tiny spark? Here's how it happens. Someone out camping in the woods forgets to thoroughly soak their campfire with water and make sure it's all the way out. The wind picks up a still-burning ember and carries it into the dry branches of a tree, and then—*pow!* A forest fire starts.

Sometimes a huge area of land is destroyed by a forest fire, and it can take years and years for the trees and plants to grow back and the animals to return. All because of a tiny spark that turned into a roaring flame.

The same kind of thing can happen in your life. Not a literal forest fire, but a fire lit by your mouth and the words you speak. Like an insult to your brother. Or some back talk to your mom. Or a rude remark to your friend. Maybe you only meant to be joking, but your words came out mean. And the other person definitely didn't take them for a joke. They took your words seriously, and now you have a big problem on your hands. Like a campfire spark igniting a dry tree branch, your destructive words are smoldering in the heart of another person.

One cruel word. One carelessly spoken sentence. One thoughtless remark. What comes from your tongue can cause a crazy amount of damage. Words can destroy friend-ships and mess up family relationships. They can give you a bad reputation—like a mean girl or a jerky guy—even if you thought you were just kidding around. Even negative words whispered to yourself can have a major effect on your confi-dence and how you feel about yourself. If you tell someone—including yourself—something enough times, it eventually begins to feel like the truth.

Can you think of a recent situation where your words hurt someone or someone else's words hurt you? What did you or the other person say? What words should or shouldn't have been spoken?

_____

_____

_____

Taming the Tongue

In the book of James, the Bible talks about animals—beasts and birds, reptiles and sea creatures. We're told that all these animals have been tamed by people. Trainers have learned how to tame lions, coax tigers to jump through hoops, teach bears to ride bikes, and convince elephants to place a foot on someone's head without crushing them.

Imagine the size of a lion, tiger, bear, or elephant. Then think about the size of a human tongue (three inches, remember?). And now, think about this. The Bible says that animals have been tamed by people, but nobody has ever figured out how to tame the tongue.

If this sounds crazy, think of how many times in the past

week you've been disciplined or scolded for the words that came out of your mouth. Try to remember any arguments you've had or words you've said that you wish you could stuff back into your mouth. You might as well add in all the times you asked yourself, *Why did I say that?*

Also, have you ever waited until your sister or your dad was out of earshot and then mumbled something about them under your breath—something you didn't want them to hear you say? Yep, that's also the sign of an untamed tongue.

What are some things you said recently that show that you need to work on taming your tongue?

_____

_____

_____

Bears can ride bikes and tigers can jump through hoops on command, but nobody can completely tame the tongue.

Part of the problem here is Satan. (He's part of every problem!) He wants nothing more than to trick you into thinking that what comes out of your mouth is no big deal and doesn't do very much damage at all. But like that spark from the campfire, a few wrong words spoken can make everything—friendships, sibling relationships, your reputation as a good leader or student or friend—go up in flames.

The Way Things Work

Would you ever go to a water fountain and assume soda will come out of it? Or bite into a burrito and expect to taste chocolate ice cream? That's not the way it works. What you see is usually what you get.

The Bible talks about this idea in the book of James: "Can both fresh water and salt water flow from the same spring? My brothers and sisters, can a fig tree bear olives, or a grape-vine bear figs? Neither can a salt spring produce fresh water" (3:11-12 NIV).

You can't go to a water fountain and out of that one opening get both fresh and salt water. You will either get fresh water or you will get salt water, but you won't get both out of the same place. And you can't go to a tree and get both olives and figs. You can only get figs from a fig tree and olives from an olive tree. In nature, things produce only what they were designed to produce. That's the way nature works.

But that's not the way the tongue works. The Bible says, "Out of the same mouth come praise and cursing" (James 3:10 NIV). This means we can speak good words and bad words—sometimes all in the same conversation. We can say things that help our friends and things that hurt them. We can even talk to ourselves two different ways. We can tell ourselves words that build us up (*You can do it!*) and words that tear us down (*You'll never be any good!*). No matter whom we're talking to, God wants us to focus on the good.

When you feel like saying negative or mean words to others (or to yourself), what are some good words you can say instead?

_____

_____

_____

THE RiGHT DiRECTiON

The rudder of a ship is a small piece of equipment attached to a huge, heavy vessel made of steel or wood. Yet that tiny piece of equipment determines the direction the boat will go. In the same way, your tongue may be small, but it will direct your life. That's the way God designed it. Use it well and keep it pointed in the right direction.

Spoken Words

When you make something—like an art project or a Lego model or even a sandwich—what part of your body do you use? You use your hands, right? Imagine trying to make any of those things with no hands. Pretty tough!

But when God created the world, He didn't roll up His sleeves and get to work. Nope. God actually created the world and all that is in it with just His words. He spoke, and that was that.

Can you imagine trying to make a peanut butter and jelly sandwich just by speaking? That would be crazy. But that's exactly what God did with the world. He demonstrated the power of spoken words when He said, "Let there be light," and there was light. The land was separated from the water not because God started digging but because God started talking. He used His mouth, not His hands.

And when the apostle John (inspired by God Himself) introduced Jesus to us in John 1:1, he said, "In the beginning was the Word, and the Word was with God, and the

Word was God." Then John went on to say in verse 14 that "the Word became flesh." When John described Jesus Christ, he talked about speech—the Word.

What are some of the things God created just by speaking them into existence? Write down as many as you can think of.

The Power of Speech

Just as God spoke everything He created into being, we too have power in our speech. That's because God gave the first human who ever walked on this earth, Adam, His word. God created Adam in His own image, and so Adam was also given the power of speech. Animals can't speak words. Plants can't speak words. The sun and moon and stars can't speak words. Only people can speak words. And while animals might be able to communicate—by meowing or barking or clucking—only people can say actual words.

As beings created in the image of the one true God, we have been given a super powerful tool in our words. Imagine how powerful speech must be if everything you see in the physical world—oceans, mountains, rivers, plants, animals—happened because of God speaking.

And God wants to keep creating in and through our mouths. That might sound a little strange, but it makes sense if you think about it. He will use your words to help you achieve the plans He has for you. And He will use your words to help other people too. He's excited to see what you can do when you start using your words for good!

WORDS THAT GIVE COURAGE

A member of the church I pastor was decorated with several medals, including the Medal of Honor, for serving in a war. In one battle, each of his men was wounded on the battlefield, and he alone went out to bring each person back to camp. Eight times he risked his own life for his men.

Where did he find this courage?

He found it in the words of his father.

Right before the man left for the war, his father took him aside and prayed with him. And then after they prayed, his father looked him in the eyes and said, "Son, I know you are coming back. I will see you again."

His father had never lied to him before, so when the man heard those words, he knew he was going to come back home alive. This belief gave him the courage to take big risks on the battlefield—risks that other men would not take—all because of the power of his father's words. When you believe in someone, their words are powerful enough to build confidence in you.

What have you learned about the power of the words we speak?

_____

_____

_____

Who are the people you tend to hurt with your words (friends, siblings, parents)?

_____

_____

_____

Write down some words you can use to build up yourself and others. (If you get stuck, think of your conversation being seasoned with salt or sweet as a honeycomb.)

_____

_____

_____

Praise the Lord with Your Words

If you've ever played sports, you know how important it is to listen to your coaches. Even when you don't agree with what they are saying, you follow their directions. If you choose to do your own thing—especially in a team sport like soccer or basketball, where everyone is supposed to be working together—you're probably going to be unhappy with the result. It might feel like the right thing to do at the time, but the coach is the one who has everything figured out and sees the big picture.

If you do your own thing in the game, everyone else has to adjust to you. And that doesn't work because you're not the one in charge. You're supposed to be out there on the court or the field doing your part for the team—passing or defending or making certain plays. The coach is the one who has trained the athletes and is watching the entire game and keeping an eye on all the players. That's why the coach needs to direct things and be the one to make adjustments.

When the coach calls for a time-out, that's when the players need to listen to their leader's words. It doesn't work if everyone is speaking at the same time, with different players giving their own ideas and feedback and nobody listening to each other. During the time-out, the players need to be silent and listen to what the coach tells them. And then they need to get back out there and put the coach's words into practice.

The Best Game Plan

Even if you don't play a sport, there is this thing called *life* that you're constantly playing. And it's not just a game. It's real. It matters. It counts.

Even though life is not a sport, it kind of helps to think about it that way. You are a player, and so is everyone else on the planet. God is the coach. But He's not just any coach, He's the best coach ever. His winning streak goes on and on. He's never lost a game, and He never will. That's the kind of coach we all wish we could play for!

Now, what do you think would happen if you refused to listen to the instructions of the winningest coach of all time? What if he told you what to do, and then you went and did the exact opposite? You would totally lose. (And your teammates probably wouldn't be very happy with you either!)

What is the result when you do your own thing and don't listen to your coach?

_____

_____

_____

What happens when you and your team *do* follow the coach's directions?

_____

_____

_____

Sadly, many people don't understand that. They like to do their own thing and make their own decisions and call their own plays. They expect everyone and everything to adjust to them—including God. But if you and God are not seeing things the same way, you would be smart to make some adjustments. God's plans never need to be improved. If you want to call your own shots, go make your own world. This is God's world, and what He says goes.

Words Matter

When you're getting directions from someone, like a coach or a teacher or a parent, you need to listen to their words. You can block out what they're saying, but you won't get the total message if you pay attention only to facial expressions, like smiles or frowns, or if you only look at body language, like hand motions and crossed arms.

Words matter. What you say is no small thing. As we learned in chapter 1 of this book, our words are powerful. They can either construct or demolish. They can be used for good or for evil. With our words, we can turn a situation in a positive direction or a negative one.

That's why it's so important for our hearts, minds, and thoughts to be connected to God and aligned with Him. If we're not connected to God, there's no telling what will come out of our mouths. Only when Jesus is Lord of our lives will He also be Lord of our lips. Our words matter, especially when we are followers of God.

YES, MASTER

Have you ever thought about what it means to call Jesus your Lord? It's kind of like calling God your Father. You might not really think about it. It's just one of those things everyone says in church or Sunday school, so you say it too.

The word "Lord" means "master." When you declare Jesus as Lord, you're saying that He's the one in control and calling the shots in your life and your speech. He's the one having the major say in your words, decisions, and actions because He is the Master.

In fact, to call Jesus "Lord" is to call yourself a servant. The job of the servant is to follow the directions of the master. As children of God, we are Christ's servants. That means we allow Him to rule our lives—we think, say, and do things that are in line with His will.

When Jesus asks us to do something, we should happily and willingly respond, "Yes, Master!" Jesus always wants what is best for us, and obeying His commands will guarantee us that we will live the best kind of life.

You've probably been in a lot of situations where a person's words have completely changed your own thoughts and attitude toward something. If you have a friend who is always complaining about stuff, you're more likely to start seeing problems all around you and to begin complaining too. If you have a teacher who's super excited about science or art or history, that excitement is contagious, and you get more interested in that subject. If you have a coach or instructor who pumps you up with positivity, you feel a lot more confident, and you start pumping up everyone around you.

Who are the people in your life whose words have an effect on your own thoughts and attitude?

_____

_____

_____

How can you use your own words to help the people around you?

_____

_____

_____

God Is Never Wrong

God wants us to listen to Him, and He also wants us to talk to Him. If we're feeling scared about a situation, He wants us to tell Him all about it. If we're feeling happy or excited or nervous or just a little unsure, He wants to know that too.

You need to be careful of one thing though. When you're listening to God and not liking what you're hearing, you should never tell Him, "Hey, God, I think You're wrong about this. I like my idea better."

Let me give you an example. Say you are having problems with a kid in your class. She just seems to be a mean person who never has anything nice to say to you—or to anyone else, for that matter. You're pretty sure God wants you to be kind and friendly to this girl. You have been reading Bible verses about being a good friend. Your Sunday school lesson was on showing kindness to others. Your parents have commented on how this girl seems to need a friend in her life. No matter where you go, you can't get away from the message of showing love and kindness to everyone. God is definitely trying to tell you something here!

But you respond to God by saying, "Hey, God, You don't get it. She's just not a nice person. I think my idea is better.

I'm just not going to talk to her. Or maybe I'll say some mean things to her just so she knows how it feels. I'm going to do this my way because I think it will work better. Besides, it's easier that way, and it's what I want to do."

If you go your own way, I can guarantee that nothing good will happen. Whenever your words are based on what you want, not what God wants, you are speaking outside of God's will. You're basically starting an argument with God, and that's one argument you never want to have. You will lose every time. It really doesn't make sense to tell God, "I think You're wrong."

The best thing to do in this situation is to begin by praising God. That might seem like a weird thing to do when you want to argue with Him. But you can totally change your mindset by saying, "Hey, God, I am struggling with this situation, so first I am going to give You praise and honor. I know that You always want what is best for me and that when I listen to You and follow Your Word, I will make good choices."

After that, tell God exactly how you're feeling about what's going on. I guarantee that when you begin by praising Him, your attitude will be completely different, and your heart will be open to what He has to say to you.

Think of a time when you wanted to do something your own way but God wanted you to do something else. What did you do? What was the result of your choice?

_____

_____

_____

Keeping It Positive

It's easy to get sucked into an argument. Most disagreements aren't even about something that matters. It's just kind of human nature to want to be first or to be right or to have our own way. And Satan wants people to argue with each other because when we're fighting, we're not focused on God or any of the positive things He wants us to be doing.

You might be arguing with a friend about the rules to a game or fighting with your brother about whose turn it is to do the dishes. And while this is going on, Satan is pumping his fist and saying, "Yes!"

What was the last thing you fought about with someone else? How did you feel when you were arguing? What can you do next time to not go there?

_____

_____

_____

Whenever you say something that disagrees with God's Word, Satan has poisoned your speech. When you complain or argue or talk about someone behind their back or just say really negative stuff, you're letting Satan have his way. And you're not keeping it positive. You're not following God.

When you agree with God and keep it positive, God will bless your words and your thoughts and your actions. If you choose to keep your focus on Him and praise His name, you'll realize that you don't really feel like arguing or fighting anymore. You have better things to do.

A Heart of Faith

Your words are simply the out-loud versions of the things you think and the things you believe. They show what is in your heart and what you are convinced is true. If your words are positive and encouraging and kind, that is what's in your heart. And if your words are negative and discouraging and unkind, well, that's what you will find in your heart. Which would you prefer?

In Hebrews 11:6, God says that without faith it is impossible to please Him but that He rewards everyone who believes in Him and seeks Him. So when God is not in control of your words, you aren't putting yourself in a very good position to please Him.

Are you pleasing God through your words? What do you think your words say about how you feel about God? What do they say about how you feel about other people? What do they say about how you feel about yourself? These are all really important questions to ask yourself.

Start thinking more about the words you choose to speak. Pay attention to what you say. Write down your words for a day if you need to (not every word, of course, but whatever you can remember). Are the words coming out of your mouth positive or negative? Are they kind or unkind? Are they true or false? What do they reflect about what's in your heart? Your goal is to develop a heart of faith and a heart that follows God. One good way to find out if you're doing this is to pay attention to your words.

Write down the words that most recently came out of your mouth. (It's okay if you have to guess; just get a general idea.)

_____

_____

_____

How do you think these words would make others feel? How did they make you feel? How do you think they make God feel?

_____

_____

_____

NO TEMPER TANTRUMS!

When you are convinced that your words have the power to invite either God or Satan into a conversation, you will naturally want to watch your mouth. But your soul, the real you on the inside, the you that no one can see, is used to getting its own way. So if you start to watch your mouth seriously, your soul is likely to throw a temper tantrum.

Did you have temper tantrums when you were

a little kid? Maybe you cried at the top of your lungs and pounded your fists and kicked your feet. You wanted your own way—and you wanted it now!

Just as small children may whine when they don't like what they have been told to do, your soul sometimes grumbles and complains when it has to do what God says rather than what you want to do. But don't worry. Your soul will adjust. A little kid eventually gets more mature and grows out of temper tantrums, and so will your soul. Just keep focusing on God—praising His name, asking Him to help you, and doing what He asks.

A Different Path

Bragging is something we've all done. Some of us tend to brag more than others, but at some point all of us have said, "Look what I did! Am I great, or what!" You might not have used those exact words, but the idea is the same— you accomplished something, and you're proud to take the credit for your success.

We all need to remember that when something works out well for us, we need to give God the glory first. He's the one who brought us the success and allowed that good thing to happen.

What good thing recently happened to you? Who got the credit—you or God?

_____

_____

_____

A big problem with taking the credit for ourselves is that we forget about God. We start to think that our own way is better than God's way. We start bragging about our abilities and all the stuff we're going to do, and we leave God out of the picture. And then when He starts leading us down a different path or asking us to do something we don't want to do, we get mad and stubborn and say, "No way am I doing that!"

Maybe you're in public school now but your parents feel like God is leading them to put you in private school. Or you're homeschooling but both of your parents have to start working full-time, and they're going to need to put you in school. You like your life the way it is. You have a ton of friends at the public school, or you like the freedom of homeschooling. But that isn't the path God has planned for you to walk—at least not right now.

You think what you want is better than what God wants. But God sees the big picture. He has the bigger plan. He knows how it's all going to work out. And so you need to trust Him. This might sound a little bit crazy, but you can even brag about Him if you aren't sure what else to do. "God, You are so awesome, I know You are going to make this work out! I'm a bit scared and a little unhappy about this, but I know You've got it covered!"

"If You Want, Lord"

It's not fun when we're doing something we like and then we get interrupted. We might be reading the best book ever or perfecting a back handspring (at last!) or drawing the coolest picture we've ever drawn—and then we're interrupted and asked to go do something else. (And it's usually something about as fun as washing dishes or pulling weeds.) We want to keep doing what we're doing, but that's not the plan.

Many of us usually don't give God very much room to interrupt. This happens when we keep doing what we want to do instead of doing what He wants us to do. But when you don't leave room for God to interrupt your life, you will be disappointed over and over again because He definitely will interrupt. After all, He's the one who controls what is going to happen. And He has ways of continuing to interrupt until He gets you to the place He was preparing for you to be. (By the way, this is an *awesome* place, and you definitely want to get there. It's definitely better than washing dishes or pulling weeds.)

You might have heard the phrase "If the Lord wills." Maybe you heard it in church or overheard an adult say it. It means the same thing as, "If You want, Lord." Which basically is you giving God permission to do something in your life. And I promise, you *do* want Him to take action and make something happen. God is in charge. God is in control. He wants to be the one controlling your words and your life, and He's the best one to do that job.

When God gets hold of your tongue, He has the rest of you too. If He can steer your speech, He can steer your life—for His glory and for your good.

Make It Public

God wants you to do more than believe what He says and just keep it to yourself. He also wants you to speak what He says. He is in charge and is ultimately in control, so let His words *to* you become your words *from* you. Matthew 10:27 (NASB) says, "What I tell you in the darkness, speak in the light; and what you hear whispered in your ear, proclaim upon the housetops."

We talk about our favorite music and movies and books and TV shows. We talk about sports and dance and art and whatever else we're into. But most of all, we should be talking about Jesus. We should be making His words public.

Jesus tells us to speak what we hear Him say. When we go out into the world—away from our family or church or Sunday school—He wants us to talk about what we have learned from Him. That amazing lesson on forgiveness, that important discussion about friendship, that small-group study about God's love...those are the things we need to be getting excited about and sharing with others.

What have you learned recently? How can you share these things with the people around you?

_____

_____

_____

Jesus does not want to be hidden in your conversation. He does not want us to be ashamed when His name is mentioned. He wants to be in the middle of our lives and the middle of our conversations. This doesn't mean we have to be saying "Jesus" every other word, but we do need to be speaking words that are positive and kind and good—the kind of words He would say. And we do need to be giving Him praise when it's time to do that.

THE QUEEN OF ENGLAND

Most of us treat Jesus the way the British treat the Queen of England. She's got a title, and everyone knows who she is; she just doesn't have much say in things. The British people recognize her and respect her, but she doesn't get to pass any laws or make any political decisions.

Do you know what the Queen of England's political role includes? One weekly meeting. Once a week, she meets with the prime minister to get an update. That's it.

Too often, we do the same with Jesus. We come to church or Sunday school once a week to get our religious update, but we don't let Jesus make any of our decisions. We don't allow Him to control our lives or influence how we speak. We call Him Lord, but we don't always let Him *be* our Lord.

But Jesus deserves a lot more than that! His words and ideas and opinions are always right, and when we follow Him, we will always do what is right and best for ourselves and for everyone around us.

Our conversations matter to God. What you say to your family or text to your friends or post online for anyone to see matters to God. We have the power to choose words that are good or evil. Our words can really make a difference—in our own lives as well as in the lives of the people around us.

So make the choice to agree with God in what you say. Make the choice to let Him be your Master and control your life and guide your decisions. The Lord is powerful, and the words He speaks are powerful as well. When you speak His Word, you gain access to that power. And...well, that's a pretty *powerful* thing!

Before you do anything or say anything, put God first. Give Him praise and tell Him, "I trust You. You've got this! I know You can make some good things happen!"

REFLECTION: YOUR WORD AND GOD'S WORD

If God is the coach of our lives, how should we respond when He asks us to do something? Why is playing the game His way better than playing it our way?

_____

_____

_____

How do you think praising God changes your mindset (the way you think)—especially when you feel like doing your own thing or getting your own way?

_____

_____

_____

How do the words you say reflect what's in your heart? What can you do to let your heart (and your words) reveal more of Jesus to the people around you?

_____

_____

_____

Be Wise with Your Words

Imagine spending a whole year learning Spanish in preparation for a really big test at the end of the year. You memorize Spanish nouns and verbs, practice putting sentences together, and speak and read the language every chance you get.

Now imagine you've reached the end of the year, and it's time for the big test...but you find out you were actually supposed to learn another language—French! Suddenly you have no clue what you're doing.

How do you think you would do on a gigantic French test if you spent all your time learning Spanish and no time at all learning French? Major fail!

When we're learning about the power of words, the same thing can happen. If we don't realize that all the study materials we need can be found in God's Word and wisdom, we're going to totally fail this thing called life. If we try to use other people or the world around us as our guide, we're not going to learn anything. All the info we need comes from God.

Being wise with our words is good for others and good for us. And the opposite is true too. When we're unwise with our words, we can hurt others and hurt ourselves. The more time we spend discovering how to use words wisely, the better chance we will have of speaking words of wisdom.

OVER A CLIFF

A super dangerous road snakes its way along part of the California coastline. It zigzags around mountains and cliffs, and sharp curves appear as suddenly as if you were playing a video game. Warning signs pop up along the way to warn drivers to slow down on the most dangerous sections and to watch out for curves, animal crossings, and falling rocks. Driving this road is pretty intense!

The signs that have been placed on California's Route 1 seem to be everywhere. But they're really important. They give drivers guidance as they make their way down the precarious highway.

Sometimes life can be like Route 1. Scary twists and turns come our way without warning.

A friend gets mad at us. A parent gets sick. We hear about terrifying things happening in the world. The more difficult and dangerous the road we're taking, the more we need warning signs and guidance. It can be hard to know how to navigate terrain with unexpected twists and turns, but God has it under control. He gives us His wisdom to help us travel safely down the highway of life.

What's Wisdom?

What do you think of when you hear the word "wisdom"? Maybe an old man stroking his long beard as he tells stories about the past. Or a brilliant teacher standing at the front of a classroom and teaching lesson after lesson. We tend to think of people being wise only if they're really old or have done a ton of schooling. But wisdom is actually available to all of us.

When you hear the word "wisdom," what image pops into your mind?

_____

_____

_____

The Bible tells us what wisdom is. We are wise when we accurately apply God's Word to the situations we deal with in life. Scripture gives us wisdom for dealing with people, dealing with ourselves, and dealing with the world. It's all in there for us to learn! Everything we need to know to live a life of wisdom can be found in the pages of the Bible.

The Opposite of Wisdom

Do you know what the opposite of wisdom is? It's foolishness. Nobody likes to be called foolish, but that's what we are if we don't learn God's wisdom and use it. Foolish people refuse to do what God says. They think their own way is better, or they simply don't want to do what God asks them to do.

The Bible often contrasts wisdom and foolishness, and one of the ways this contrast shows up the most is with regard to our speech, as in this verse from the book of Proverbs: "The tongue of the wise makes knowledge attractive, but the mouth of fools blurts out foolishness" (15:2).

Lots of verses in Proverbs talk about the wise and the foolish, which kind of gives you the idea that you speak and act either one way or the other. There's no in between. Pick one—wise or foolish. It might sound kind of extreme, but it's true. If you choose to speak words that are from God's heart and mind, you're choosing wisdom. Anything that goes against what God would have you say is foolishness.

Think back on your day. What words of wisdom have you spoken? (They don't have to be super brilliant words; just think of things God would be proud to hear you say.)

_____

_____

_____

Now think about any foolish words you said. What were they? What can you do to choose words of wisdom next time?

_____

_____

_____

God makes it clear in His Word that if we are wise with our speech, life will be better for us. When we are foolish with our speech, life doesn't go as well.

Think about the times when you've thought to yourself, *Why did I say that?* or *I can't believe those words just came out of my mouth!* Sometimes you need to stop a minute before you say anything and ask yourself, *How can I speak words of wisdom instead of words of foolishness? What would Jesus want me to say in this situation?* Don't worry about looking stupid when you hesitate before you speak. In most situations, it actually makes you look smarter!

Talk better, and you will live better.

The Secret Formula

If someone told you there was a secret formula for getting straight A's in school, would you want to know what it was? Of course you would!

God has given us a secret formula for getting wisdom. Are you ready for it?

Knowledge + Understanding = Wisdom

Just two ingredients: knowledge and understanding. That's the secret formula. Right there. All you need to know.

Knowledge

Have you ever been talking to someone when suddenly, halfway through the conversation, you get some new information that totally changes the way you think about what's going on? Maybe a friend is telling you a story about something that happened, and once you get the new information, you are able to understand what happened in a new way. Or the reason someone did something or said something totally makes sense now. It's like viewing a picture that suddenly comes into focus. "Oh, I get it!" you say. "Now that makes sense!"

When you don't know exactly what is going on—when you don't have the *knowledge*—you don't have wisdom. Without knowledge, you don't completely get what is going on. And if you don't get what is going on, you might be tempted to think or say or do the wrong thing.

God tells us, "The fear of the LORD is the beginning of wisdom, and the knowledge of the Holy One is understanding" (Proverbs 9:10). That's why you need to get all the information you can before you make a decision or respond to a situation. And you get that information—or knowledge—from God's truth.

Have you ever just *known* that something is true or that someone is right? That's the kind of knowledge we're talking about here. You can count on it. It's been proven to be true. There's no room for doubt. When you start with God, you can be sure that your information is accurate. You can be certain that you have *knowledge*.

Understanding

The second part of the secret formula for wisdom is

understanding. Proverbs 4:7 says, "Wisdom is supreme—so get wisdom. And whatever else you get, get understanding." Knowledge has to do with information, but understanding has to do with the meaning of the information. When you are able to combine knowledge and understanding together, you end up with wisdom.

Think back to the conversation with your friend. The story your friend told you was a little bit confusing before you got more information—the *knowledge*. But you can only *understand* the story if you know stuff about your friend and the situation and maybe the other people involved. And to understand something, you have to want to understand it. You have to make an effort.

What is the secret formula for getting wisdom?

_____

_____

_____

One more thing: Wisdom is more than being smart. You can get straight A's and still act foolishly. Wisdom is being able to actually *use* God's words of truth when you're with your friends or family, in school or at your activities—wherever you find yourself in life. Wisdom is making the best choice, the one that will bring about the best result for everyone involved. Wisdom is doing what Jesus would want you to do.

PICK A PARACHUTE

Four desperate people were on an airplane that had lost an engine and was about to go down. Unfortunately, there were only three parachutes on the plane. The pilot was the first one to grab a parachute and jump—he said he had a wife and two kids, so he needed to live. Next was a man who was known as a genius. He looked at the other two people and said he needed to live so the world could benefit from his brilliant mind.

This left a minister and a kid in the airplane. The minister turned to the kid and said, "I've lived a full life. I'm not afraid to die and meet God." With that, he offered the parachute to the kid.

The kid just smiled and said, "That's okay, sir. There are still two parachutes left—the genius just grabbed my backpack and jumped."

You can be smart but not know the difference between a parachute and a backpack. You need both knowledge and understanding if you want to have wisdom.

Dealing with Foolishness

Even if you choose the way of wisdom, you're going to have to deal with a lot of foolishness in this world. Your siblings might make fun of you. Kids at school sometimes say mean things. People will try to convince you to do stuff you know you shouldn't do. What happens then? How do you react? Which words should come out of your mouth?

A foolish mouth is one of the most destructive things on the planet. You can always apologize for something you say, but you can never take it back. It's impossible to go back in time and start over. That's why you need to watch your words—including your responses.

The Bible says that when someone speaks words of foolishness to us, we shouldn't make a big deal about it. Instead, we should answer that person simply: "Answer a fool according to his own foolishness or he'll become wise in his own eyes" (Proverbs 26:5). This means you shouldn't get into an argument or even try to prove you're right. Instead, respond with wisdom and kindness. And then change the subject or start talking to someone else. It's often better just not to go there and get involved when you see foolish behavior.

When someone else's words bother you, ask yourself if that person is choosing the best way. Are they speaking the way God would have them speak? Are their words helpful, or are they hurtful? If their words go against God and what you know is right, it's time to move on. Don't hang out with someone whose words will influence you the wrong way or bring you down. Yes, you can be nice to that person, but be careful.

When was the last time someone spoke words of foolishness to you? How did you respond? How can you respond more wisely next time?

_____

_____

_____

Go Ahead and Be Greedy!

When it comes to some things—like candy or video games or the latest clothes or shoes—wanting more and more isn't a good thing. Eating too much candy will make you feel sick. Playing too many video games will fry your brain. Worrying about wearing certain brands will stress you out. In this world, being greedy isn't usually the best thing.

But it's okay to be greedy with wisdom. We *should* be seeking more and more of it. As we grow in our relationship with God, we should be asking Him for more and more wisdom. In fact, every day we should try to get more wisdom than we had the previous day.

Wisdom can guide us through life the way someone can lead us up a steep and dangerous mountain. Wisdom can steer us through the pathways of life, telling us where to make a turn and where not to make a turn, what to choose and what not to choose, what person is helping and what person is not helping. Wisdom can be an awesome guide!

Wisdom shows us the right words to say and the correct things to do. When we're scared or nervous about something, wisdom shows us how to respond. When our friends or family members are having trouble, wisdom shows us how to help them. Even when life is going great and everything seems perfect, wisdom shows us what to do. We always need wisdom, so we should be greedy about getting it!

What are some things that people are greedy about getting? Do you think these are good things or bad things? Why is it okay to be greedy about getting wisdom?

_____

_____

_____

Where Is Wisdom?

So where is wisdom, anyway? It would be nice if we could go to the store and buy a box of wisdom, but it's actually simpler than that. It doesn't take any money to get wisdom. You don't have to drive somewhere to go get it. You don't have to be a certain age to purchase it. It's available right now for anyone who wants it.

If you were to go on a search for wisdom right now, where would you look first?

_____

_____

_____

Sometimes people look for wisdom in others or in nature, but those things aren't the true source of wisdom. You might find information or inspiration in those things, but you will not find the guidance you need to make right choices.

The true source of wisdom is God. He established wisdom. He creates it. He defines it. God alone is wisdom, just as God alone is love. Apart from God, wisdom does not exist. That's because God knows everything and is the only One who does.

If you want to find wisdom, you first need to find God. Learn all you can about Him. Read the Bible. Memorize verses so you have them in your heart at all times. Go to church and Sunday school and youth group. Ask more mature Christians about their faith and the things they have learned. Pray and talk to God. Ask Him to give you more and more wisdom. If you do these things, I can promise you that you will become super rich in wisdom!

What can you do in your life right now to get more and more wisdom?

_____

_____

_____

The Gift of Wisdom

Wisdom is so valuable that gold cannot be exchanged for it, nor can it be bought. This might make it sound like wisdom is impossible to get, but wisdom is actually free. All you need is a heart that seeks it.

And while wisdom is free if you ask for it, it isn't always easy to get in our world. Sometimes it's hard to do the right thing—especially when you seem to be the only one doing it. Everyone else is reading a book or watching a TV show that your parents don't want you to read or watch. Everyone else is using certain words that you know God wouldn't want you to say. Everyone else is talking back or making fun of others or being exclusive, and you know deep down that you aren't supposed to do those things.

But when you honestly seek God's wisdom and let Him work in your heart and your life, really amazing stuff will happen! You'll hear yourself say something or respond to someone in a way you never could have on your own. And the more this happens, the more you'll want to rely on God and do things His way and with His wisdom. Before you know it, your first move will be to check with God before opening your mouth.

God is willing to give you wisdom when you ask, so why not ask for it? It's like a teacher saying, "Hey! I have all the correct answers to the test. Do you want them?" You would be crazy to say no!

What are some situations in your life (with your friends or family or at school) where you could use more of God's wisdom? Write down a prayer to ask Him to give you wisdom in these things.

_____

_____

_____

WISE SOLUTIONS

One day a son went to his father with a problem. He had loaned a friend $500, but his friend had not yet paid him back. So much time had passed, he thought his friend had actually forgotten. No paper was signed, and he had given his friend cash, so he was concerned that he wouldn't be able to prove his friend owed him the money.

"That's not a problem," his dad replied. "Just text your friend that you'd like the $1000 you loaned him back. When he texts you back that it was only $500, you've got it in writing!"

When you ask a wise person for wisdom, you will get solutions where you thought there were none. (And you will probably get your money back!)

A Daily Habit

You have daily habits, right? Like eating breakfast. Brushing your teeth. Feeding your pets. Taking care of the things you need to take care of.

Write down some of your daily habits—the things you do (or are supposed to do!) every day.

_____

_____

_____

Now, what happens when you forget to do these daily things? If you don't eat breakfast, you get super hungry and probably kind of grumpy! If you don't brush your teeth, you get bad breath and maybe eventually some cavities. Not fun! If you don't feed your pets, they meow or bark until they get some food.

Another one of your daily habits should be asking God for His wisdom to guide your words. You don't have to make it a long prayer—just a sincere one. And after you ask, pay attention to all the ways God guides you and helps you.

Remember, your words matter. They can help or hurt people. Even if you think you're just joking around, the other person might not take it that way. Think about how you might feel if someone spoke the same words to you. Ask yourself if Jesus would be proud of you for speaking those words. (By the way, joking around is just fine. It's one of the ways friends have fun together. But you need to make sure it doesn't cross the line to being mean.)

God really does want to give you His wisdom. He knows how valuable it is, and He knows how much better your life will be if you seek His way and His words. God wants you to be wise—to have both knowledge and understanding (remember the secret formula?)—so that your words bring glory to Him, good to others, and blessing to yourself.

Words of wisdom—you've got this!

REFLECTION: YOUR WORD AND GOD'S WORD

Where does all the wisdom in the world come from? How can you get this wisdom?

_____

_____

_____

What is the difference between a wise person and a foolish person?

_____

_____

_____

What are some words of wisdom others have spoken to you? What are some words of wisdom you can speak that will help others?

_____

_____

_____

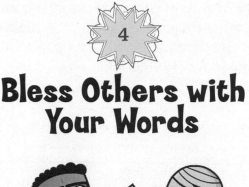

4

Bless Others with Your Words

f you've ever seen a building being demolished, you've seen how quickly something can come down. What takes years to construct can be destroyed in a matter of days. It's impressive—and a little bit scary when the building implodes.

Just as an implosion takes only minutes to bring down what took years to build, our words have the power to destroy other people and even ourselves as soon as they're spoken. That's why we need to be so careful with our words. And that's why we need to learn to use our words to build and not to tear down. We can use our words to build good friendships. We can use our words to strengthen our relationships with our parents and siblings. We can even use our words to help people we don't know very well. Our words have amazing power to bless others!

Build Up

If you've played on a team or been in a group where everyone was encouraging everyone else and saying super positive stuff, you know how helpful that is. When other people have confidence in you, you have confidence in yourself. You might not be totally sure you can play that clarinet solo or make that soccer goal or perform your dance without forgetting the choreography, but when someone says, "You've got this!" it completely ups your confidence. If someone else believes you can do it, you probably can! And that attitude is contagious. Pretty soon, everyone in the group is feeling confident about their abilities. And it shows in how everyone performs in the concert or the game or the dance.

Think of a time when you weren't sure you could do something. What did someone else tell you that gave you the confidence to try it—and succeed?

_____

_____

_____

What are some words you can say to others when they aren't so sure they can accomplish something?

_____

_____

_____

The Bible is filled with verses that tell us to build each other up. Here are two examples:

- "We must pursue what promotes peace and what builds up one another" (Romans 14:19).
- "Encourage one another and build each other up as you are already doing" (1 Thessalonians 5:11).

God tells us to love Him and love others. One of the best ways we can show our love for others is by encouraging them and building them up.

Open Your Mouth

I'm sure you've heard someone tell you to close your mouth—like when you're caught talking in class or arguing with your brother or even chewing food with your mouth open (yuck!). But sometimes you are supposed to *open* your mouth. One of those times is when you have an opportunity to build up someone.

And it's not just the words you say out loud. It's the words you send in a text message. Or the words you post online. Or the words you whisper in someone's ear. Or even the words you think to yourself. All those words matter!

When the people in your home, at your school, in your church, at your activities, or in your neighborhood talk to you and hang out with you, do they sense that you are building them up, or do they feel as if you're tearing them down? After they spend time with you, do you think they feel better about themselves, or do they feel worse? And—this is the most important part—do you think they can see Jesus in you?

It's also not just saying good things. Yes, you should try to make your words positive and encouraging. But it's also about what you *don't* say. You've probably heard the saying, "If you can't say something nice, don't say anything at all." And that's really true! Sometimes you need to stop yourself before letting hurtful or unkind words escape from your mouth.

Ephesians 4:29 (NASB) says, "Let no unwholesome word proceed from your mouth, but only such a word as is good for edification according to the need of the moment, so that it will give grace to those who hear." The word "edification" means building each other up. We do that by what we say and how we say it, as well as what we choose *not* to say.

Think About It

Words that people speak to each other matter a lot. How many times have you repeated something in your head that someone said to you earlier that day or that week? Maybe your friend jokingly called you clumsy when you tripped and fell, and that word "clumsy" kept popping back into your mind when you messed up in your soccer game or couldn't learn the new step in tap class. Or your teacher made a remark about you needing to study harder for the next test, and suddenly you felt as if you're not a very good student. These words weren't intended to be hurtful, but sometimes you can't help but take them that way. That's why you need to be careful and really think about what you say to others.

What words did someone say to you this week that you keep replaying in your mind? How did these words make you feel?

_____

_____

_____

NOTHING TO SAY

Someone once shared that when she decided to give up gossip, she literally had nothing to say to herself or her friends for three full weeks. Gossip was pretty much all that had been coming out of her mouth, and she had to relearn how to talk about other things.

Think about the conversations you've had with your friends recently. Have you spent the time talking about other people and passing on information you shouldn't pass on? Have the majority of your conversations been about who said what and who did what and who's friends with whom and who's not friends with whom?

If the answer is yes, there's a pretty good chance you've been spending your time gossiping.

Even if you don't think you're gossiping, ask yourself how many of the words coming out of your mouth are put-downs or sarcastic comments that hurt others. Those things can be just as bad as gossip.

Relearning how to talk can be hard at first. But eventually you'll get in the habit of saying good things and having fun and positive communication. The best part? You won't have to worry about what you say!

Our words can really affect the way people feel about themselves—and they can affect the way we feel about ourselves too. If you've ever just blurted out the first thing that popped into your mind and then realized it didn't come out right, you know what I mean. This can be a hard thing if you're the kind of person who likes to talk a lot! It can also be hard if you have trouble figuring out what to say.

It's a lot to take in, but just remember one thing: The purpose of the mouth is to build up. If you're unsure of what to say, ask yourself, *How would I feel if someone said this to me?* If you're still unsure, it's probably best not to say anything at all.

Salty in a Good Way

Have you ever had food when the cook accidentally left out the salt? From cookies to mashed potatoes to hot dogs, salt is a majorly essential ingredient in a lot of recipes. (Can you imagine potato chips without salt? No way!)

What foods would taste terrible without salt? (If you're not sure how important salt is, go check the labels of some of your favorite foods or look in a cookbook!)

_____

_____

_____

The Bible says, "Your speech should always be gracious, seasoned with salt, so that you may know how you should answer each person" (Colossians 4:6). God uses the word "always" to remind us how often our speech should be seasoned with grace—*all the time!*

Just as salt can change the taste of a French fry, turning it from plain potato to something incredible, graciousness can turn your speech into something remarkable. And what exactly is graciousness? A gracious person is kind and thoughtful and helpful. A gracious person thinks of others—what they need and how they might feel. A gracious person is the best kind of friend!

If you've ever watched a cooking show, you've probably seen someone leave out an essential seasoning, such as salt. When the seasoning is left out, the dish tastes bland or just plain yucky. Good cooks use seasoning knowingly, and they often taste what they're cooking to determine how much seasoning to use. A master chef will season the food and then taste it, going back and forth until it is just right. God wants you and me to do the same with our speech—to make it tasty and life-giving to those who hear it. To do that, we sometimes need to go back and forth until it's just right.

How to Speak Graciously

By now you know that your speech needs to be seasoned with grace, but what does that mean exactly? First, we need to think about God's grace. He is loving and kind to us, even when we don't deserve it. He gives us second chances, even when we don't deserve them. He is patient and forgiving with us, even when we don't deserve those things. Stop for a minute to think about this. Let God's awesome grace wash over you for a few moments.

Now, imagine yourself passing on God's grace to others. Picture yourself treating people with love and kindness. Imagine yourself giving someone a second chance. See yourself being patient and forgiving with others. And when you're doing this, pay careful attention to the words you speak. Ask God to tell you what to say and how to say it, because it can be really hard to get those things right. It can be super tempting to react to stuff right away with our words, but what we often need to do instead is stop, take a few deep breaths, and tell God, *Help! I have no clue what to do here!*

And that's exactly what God wants us to do. He's always there to help. Because He is gracious, God will help us know how to respond—with grace.

CHOOSING GRACE

People used to season some foods with salt to prevent them from decaying. Similarly, speech that is flavored with grace prevents decay in our relationships, dreams, and much more. Gracious speech preserves everyone involved.

When you are not preserving something through what you say, you are contributing to its decay. You can choose to use your mouth for good or for evil—those are your only options. God has set it up that way. Your words will create good or bring in evil whether you are aware of it or not. Make the choice to flavor your speech with grace and to create good.

How You Say It

Okay, you're going to be totally familiar with this one: *How you say something is often just as important as what you say.* When your mom or dad asks you to do a chore and you snap back, "Fine! I'll do it!" that can actually be worse than simply forgetting to do the chore. Your negative attitude affects everyone who hears you, and pretty soon your parent is mad at you, you're grumpy, and everyone around you is in a bad mood.

Or your best friend just got a new pair of shoes, but you think they are super ugly. Instead of pleasantly saying, "I couldn't really wear those shoes, but they totally work on you!" you roll your eyes and say, "There is no way I would ever wear shoes like that." Is the meaning the same? Pretty much. The shoes aren't for you. But is your friend going to take what you say in a very different way, depending on how you say it? Definitely!

Some people are too direct in their speech. They blurt out whatever is on their mind without stopping to think about how it will make others feel. Other people are sneaky and whispery and gossipy. That can sometimes be worse than being too direct.

Take a minute to consider what kind of speaker you are. Is there room for you to soften what you say? Are you perfecting the art of being polite when you talk to the people around you? How can you change your tone or your mood so that what you say comes out better? Sometimes just remembering to smile when you say something will do the trick!

Think of a time when you said something that didn't come out right and someone got upset with you. What happened? How could you have said it differently?

_____

_____

_____

Too Thirsty

How do you feel after eating a bunch of potato chips, or a handful of snack mix, or mashed potatoes with lots of butter and salt? You feel thirsty, right? That's another thing about salt—it makes you thirsty. Suddenly you *need* a giant glass of water! The more salty food you eat, the more water you want.

The same thing is true with your words. When you choose to season your speech with God's grace, people will come back to you thirsty to hear more. They will want to listen to your words, and your voice will make others feel good about themselves and about others. Win, win!

When God sees you working hard to make your speech positive and encouraging, He will help you with your words. Here's a good prayer to pray: *Lord, please make Your words my words. Speak through me, and help me say the things You want me to say.*

God is a God of grace, so if you're speaking without grace, He won't participate in your communication. He doesn't want any part of it. You'll be on your own when you choose to ignore how God wants you to speak. But when you invite God into your words, mouth, language, and conversation, He's all in. He will help you speak those words that are filled with salt, which will make others thirsty to hear more.

Words That Help Others

One of the best things we can do is speak words that help others. You know how you feel when you get a bad grade or are coming down with a cold or are just sad. The little things people say, like "You've got this," or "Do you want to talk?" or "It will be okay" can make a major difference. It's not even the words that are spoken. It's that they were spoken at all. Someone sees you. Someone cares. Someone wants to help.

Remember back to the last bad day you had or the last thing that went wrong. Who spoke some words that helped you feel better? What did that person say?

_____

_____

_____

Even in really hard situations where you don't know what to say—like if your friend's parents are getting divorced or someone's grandparent just died—God can give you words of grace that will really help the other person. God will honor you for using your words, your texts, your social media posts, and your prayers to remind others to hope in Him. He can use your words to help others turn to Him. That's really cool, isn't it?

TEXT MESSAGES FROM GOD

One time when I had been having a lot of doubts and wondering whether I was doing a very good job with a lot of things, I asked God, *Does what I'm doing really matter?*

God knew how I was feeling, and something really cool happened next. Someone who cared about me began texting me every Sunday morning. The texts were never long, but they always included an encouraging Bible verse. That meant so much to me!

I felt as if God Himself were texting me, reminding me that what I did made a difference and encouraging me to hang in there, to keep going, and to continue doing what He had called me to do. You never know how powerful your words can be in someone else's life!

Sometimes God will prompt you to say or send something to someone without even really knowing what's going on in that person's life. It's not important that you know what's going on. God knows, and He knows that you can be the right person to offer a word of encouragement or understanding. Proverbs 25:11 is such a great verse: "A word spoken at the right time is like gold apples on a silver tray."

The Good Kind of Gossip

Okay...that heading is a little misleading. Gossip isn't usually a good thing. But did you know that there's a good way of talking about others behind their back? We can call it the *good* kind of gossip—the kind you wouldn't mind getting back to the person you're talking about.

Everyone likes to be spoken of highly. Don't you like the idea of other people saying nice and positive things about you? We all do!

When you're talking about someone else, always try to include a positive statement about that person. "Maddie is such a great dancer." "Brandon always makes me laugh." "Taylor is super smart." You can even do this when you're introducing that person to someone else. Try making this a habit in your life and relationships.

This habit works really well in a lot of situations. For example, it's a great way to stop mean gossip. When other kids are putting down someone or making fun of them behind their backs or sending nasty texts, all you need to do is say just one nice thing about the person they're talking about. Even something like "Diego has always been a good friend to me." That one positive statement causes others to stop, take notice, and maybe realize that they've gone too far. Just one nice comment can turn things around.

What are some ways you can spread positive gossip and stop negative gossip in its tracks?

_____

_____

_____

Be All There

Have you ever been with a group of friends when everyone was staring at their phones but nobody was talking to each other? It happens all the time! I guess everyone could be texting nice things to others, but it's way better to actually talk to the people you're with and be all there. You're going to remember laughter and personal conversation way more than you're going to remember text strings and emojis, and you connect way better with other people when you're actually hanging out together.

Being present is a lost art in our world. Instead of being together, people actually are going somewhere else when they pick up their phones or tablets. And they're basically telling the people they're with, "Something else is more important than spending time with you."

I'm a pastor, so imagine how weird it would be if I stood up to preach but then got out my phone and started texting someone or reading posts on social media. That would be rude—not to mention kind of crazy! Yet how many times do we sit down to lunch or dinner with our family or friends and casually pick up our phones and go somewhere else? That's not okay either!

When you spend time with people, make sure to put away any distractions and give the people you're with your full attention. *Be all there.* And despite what you or others might think, being constantly on your phone is not a sign that you are oh so important. It's actually a sign of low self-esteem. You're saying that you don't value yourself enough to believe you have something to offer those around you.

But you *do* have value—tons of it! God values you. And He values others. Because of this awesome truth, we need to value each other and be there—*all* there—for each other.

Think of the last time you and your friends or family hung out together. What distractions kept you from connecting with each other? What can you do differently next time?

_____

_____

_____

Share the Love

When it comes to saying the right words to others, some people seem to think it's more important to tell the truth than to share the love. But the Bible says that we are supposed to do both of these things: "Speaking the truth in love, let us grow in every way into Him who is the head—Christ" (Ephesians 4:15).

Let your words contain both truth and love. If something is true but it doesn't share love, you might want to think twice before you say it. Criticisms and put-downs often fall into this category. Also, sometimes we think something is true based on what we've heard, but it turns out not to be true at all. For example, you've heard that the new girl at school is really stuck up. But when you actually get to know her, you realize that she's not stuck up at all. In fact, she's incredibly nice.

Here's something else to keep in mind. When you tell someone the truth without caring about them, they might react negatively to your conversation. They can tell that you aren't coming from a place of love, so your words aren't going to matter much to them. After all, why should they believe someone who doesn't seem to care about them?

Share the Truth

You also can't have love without truth. Remember, God is love. And God is truth. You need both!

Your words might make people feel good about themselves for a moment, but if they aren't true, you shouldn't say them at all. If you don't tell someone the truth, you don't help them. Sometimes you have to risk having people get mad at you for telling the truth (that happened to Jesus all the time!), but God always rewards telling the truth when you back up your words with love.

It takes some practice, but the best way to build other people up is to combine truth and love so that the people listening to your words receive the right information from the right heart. When you're not sure whether to say something, ask yourself two questions: *Is it true? Is it kind?* If the answer to either of those questions is no, you probably shouldn't say anything. If the answer is definitely yes, go for it!

What two questions should you ask yourself when you're not sure whether you should say something?

_____

_____

_____

Word Power

Your words are so important, and they can help other people so much. Your words can help your mom feel better after a rough day at work. They can encourage a friend to keep working toward his goals. They can make just one person laugh and smile—and then that person makes someone else laugh and smile, and pretty soon the mood of an entire group has changed for the better. That's word power!

The Bible says that speaking is actually a ministry. When our language "is good for building up someone in need...it gives grace to those who hear" (Ephesians 4:29). The person hearing your words may not necessarily deserve the grace you're giving them, but that's exactly why it's called grace. And that's exactly what God gives to us in so many ways— His grace—so we need to turn around and give that grace to others. Words of encouragement. Truthful compliments. Positive "gossip" about other people. Words that build up instead of tear down.

Words are powerful tools. Play with them this week—in a good way! When you are tempted to say something mean or hurtful to someone, do the opposite and say something kind and helpful. When you really want to gossip and talk about someone behind her back, instead say one or two nice things about her. When you are tempted to lie, tell the truth instead—with plenty of love. Then watch and see what Jesus does in your life. It will be incredible!

When you ask God for help with your words, He will always help you. He is faithful. As you serve Him by using His words to build up others, you will begin to see His plan for your life more and more. You'll realize all the amazing ways He uses His followers—including you—to do good things in the world. So speak up—and build up! Use your words to bless others.

REFLECTION: YOUR WORD AND GOD'S WORD

What are some ways you can use your words to build up others? Think of everyone you see—your family, your friends, your neighbors, and anyone else you talk to during the day. Your words can encourage all these people!

_____

_____

_____

What does it mean to speak with grace? What does God teach us about speaking graciously?

_____

_____

_____

What does it mean to share the truth? What does it mean to share the love? Why is it so important to share truth and love together?

_____

_____

_____

Be Thankful with Your Words

Sometimes it seems like just about anyone can be famous. Normal, ordinary people get cast on reality shows, start YouTube channels, or develop a major following on social media. But to be a true celebrity, you need fame, power, a special ability, an important position, or money. Only a small percentage of people are actual celebrities, and sometimes their fame lasts for only a short time.

The greatest celebrity of all, though, has always been known and will always be known. He is the celebrity of the universe in His own unique way. He's not like modern-day celebrities—popular one year and then forgotten the next. Nobody is greater than this celebrity, and no one can ever take His place.

You've probably guessed by now that the greatest celebrity of all time is God. He never loses His status. His gifts and skills never fade away. He was famous well before the internet ever existed, and He will always be known. His message is always relevant. He is forever the Almighty One.

Your Favorite Celebrity

If you found out you were going to meet your favorite celebrity, you would want to be prepared, wouldn't you? You would decide ahead of time what you would wear, what you would say, and how you would act. And you'd probably be a little bit nervous! You would want to make a good impression.

What would you do if you found out you were going to meet your favorite celebrity of all time? Who would that be? How would you get ready for your meeting?

_____

_____

_____

Every day, you have the chance to interact with the best-known celebrity of all-time—God. And you don't have to figure out all on your own how to act. You don't need to be nervous about your meeting. The Bible gives us plenty of directions about what to do. Here's one of the most important directions: "Give thanks in everything, for this is God's will for you in Christ Jesus" (1 Thessalonians 5:18).

That's a pretty clear instruction: "Give thanks in everything." When we use our words to talk to God, we need to keep this instruction in mind. It's simple to do, but it's not always easy. It's kind of like treating your sister with kindness. You know how to be kind, but you don't always do it. Fortunately, there are many ways to give thanks—as well as many things for which to be thankful.

What Is Thanksgiving?

When you hear the word "thanksgiving," you might think of a holiday in November when you get together with your family and eat way too much turkey, cranberry sauce, stuffing, and pumpkin pie. But that's not the kind of thanksgiving we're talking about here.

What pops into your mind when you hear the word "thanksgiving"?

_____

_____

_____

What does it mean to give thanks to God? When you give God thanksgiving, you don't give Him an extra helping of stuffing or a second piece of pumpkin pie. You use your words and your actions to recognize His goodness. You give Him your gratitude for being the source of all the good things in your life. It's easy to give thanks when you remember that God is the One behind every opportunity, every blessing, and every good thing in your life.

It's also easy to give our thanks to other people—or even to ourselves. When we get awesome grades or we improve a ton in our sport or we land a really big part in a play, we tend to congratulate ourselves. While it's true that we did work hard and put in the effort, we need to always remember to thank God for our success. Because without Him, we aren't capable of doing anything at all. He is the One who created us and gave us our gifts and talents.

Go ahead and thank your teachers and coaches and parents and instructors. And remember, it's okay to be proud of yourself. God and others are proud of you too. But always be sure to give thanks to God as well!

THANK YOU!

As soon as children learn to speak, their parents teach them the importance of saying thank you. God's heart desires the same from us. Thanksgiving includes more than the words you say. You don't say "thanks" one time in the morning and then consider yourself good for the rest of the day. How would your parents feel if you thanked them one time for everything they have done and will ever do for you, but then you never thanked them again?

God wants our hearts to beat with thanksgiving for Him. He wants us to give Him thanks all day long as we see the amazing things He does in our lives. The words "thank you" should always be coming out of our mouths. When we feel happy, we should say thank you. When we're having fun with our friends, we should say thank you. When we see the amazing world that God created, we should say thank you. The more you notice, the more you will realize how much you have to be thankful for!

Don't Reject Anything

You've probably said, "No, thanks" to some of the dishes on your family's Thanksgiving table. Maybe you're allergic to dairy, so you can't eat the mashed potatoes Aunt Susan made with butter. Or maybe you just don't care for the brussels sprouts casserole that Uncle Jesse always insists on bringing. A polite "No, thank you," is just fine. You don't need to make a big deal out of it. You just pass the dish on to the next person.

It's different with the things God gives us. We aren't supposed to reject anything. The Bible says, "Everything created by God is good, and nothing should be rejected if it is received with thanksgiving" (1 Timothy 4:4).

We are to receive everything God gives us with a heart of thanks. Nothing is to be rejected if it comes from God's own hand. That's because nothing that comes from God is gross (like Uncle Jesse's brussels sprouts casserole) or bad for you. James 1:17 says, "Every generous act and every perfect gift is from above, coming down from the Father of lights."

Everything good in our lives ultimately comes from God,

and things go better when we recognize this. Yes, it's important to thank other people when they give us something or help us with something. It's also okay to be proud of yourself when you have worked hard to achieve something. Just don't take anything away from God. In the end, remember that He is the source of all the blessings and achievements and accomplishments in your life.

What are some things you can thank God for right now? Look around you and write down as many as you can think of.

_____

_____

_____

Many Words

Can you think of some other ways to say thank you? Maybe you can say, "I appreciate it" or "That means a lot to me." But mainly, we just say, "Thank you."

Here's something kind of crazy: The Old Testament in the Bible was written in Hebrew, and it has no Hebrew word that specifically means "thank you." We tend to say a short and simple thank you to express our gratitude to God. But the Hebrews thanked Him by speaking tons and tons of words. Just one word couldn't express all their appreciation. It was too big, too powerful, too deep.

One of those words was *yadah*. It literally means to talk about how wonderful someone is or to go on and on about a great thing they did. The Israelites liked to thank someone by spreading a good report about that person. It's kind of like that good "gossip" we talked about in chapter 4. You brag on a person. You don't shut up about how awesome they are and the amazing things they did. That's one great way to say thanks to God.

Another Hebrew word that communicates thanks in the Old Testament is the word we often translate as "hallelu-jah," which you have probably heard in worship songs sung in church. Hallelujah is a combination of two words: *hallalu*, which means "praise," and *Jah*, which is short for Yahweh (another name for God). Put together, these words mean, "Praise God!"

The Power of Praise

We shout out our praise for a sports team that just won a big game, and we wildly applaud for celebrities when we see them. We should also shout out our praises to God and applaud for Him. That's what His heart desires and what He deserves. After all, the ordinary things God does are way more incredible than the extraordinary things people do.

What are some of the ways you can praise God? How do you see people praising God in church, at home, and in other parts of your life?

_____

_____

_____

The Bible tells us we are supposed to use our words to praise God. "I will praise the LORD at all times; His praise will always be on my lips" (Psalm 34:1). The New American

Standard Bible puts it this way: "His praise shall continually be in my mouth."

The word "continually" means all the time. No stopping. No pausing. Ever. Of course, it would be impossible to keep saying thank you out loud without ever taking a breath. But God never has to be far from your thoughts. When you see a breathtaking sunset, think of Him and thank Him. When you receive a pile of birthday presents, think of Him and thank Him (and of course, thank the people who gave you the presents!). When you've having a blast riding roller coasters at Disneyland or paddling a canoe across a lake, think of Him and thank Him.

God is blessed by your words of appreciation. He wants to hear your gratitude and thanksgiving. You bless Him when you remember what He has done for you and express your gratefulness to Him and to others. Let the words "thank you" be always in your heart and on your lips.

BE THANKFUL... OR ELSE!

I used to have a dog. I fed that dog faithfully. I changed the water in its bowl every single day. That dog never once told me thanks. In fact, one time when I went to feed the dog, he growled at me as I set the food bowl down next to him. Which is exactly why I started this story with "I *used* to have a dog." Things don't work that way in my house. If you want to stay in my house, no growling is allowed, and you better come with some thanks.

Now that's just me, a human being. Can you imagine how God must feel when He constantly gives us good things—day in and day out—and rarely gets thanked? Then, when we feel as if something has gone wrong, we growl and complain at the One who has done so much for us and is continuing to do so much more!

So be sure to watch your mouth. Be thankful...or else!

Replace Complaining with Being Grateful

It's totally natural to want to complain about things. A mean teacher. The rain that never stops. The annoying things your little brother does. We tend to complain without even realizing that we're complaining. When we sigh deeply or mutter "ugh" or simply have a bad attitude about whatever we're doing, that's complaining.

Write down all the things you want to complain about. Don't hold back—write down everything!

_____

_____

_____

Now, write down how you feel after complaining about everything.

_____

_____

_____

It's easy to find things to complain about. So easy that complaining can actually become kind of addictive. And it can be contagious. One person complains, then another person adds to the complaining, and before you know it, everyone is complaining. It's like a big complain-fest! And all that complaining leaves everyone unhappy and irritable. Suddenly, everyone—including you—is in a bad mood. Not fun!

When you find yourself complaining or you're with a group of people who are complaining, make a big effort to replace complaining with thanksgiving. Complaining doesn't just make us unhappy. It distances us from God. And when we find ourselves far away from God, we miss out on many of the blessings He had prepared for us, and we experience His discipline instead.

Imagine you're on a trip to Disneyland, and there are a lot of rides and shows and foods you want to enjoy. But you get in a really bad mood for some reason. You start complaining and arguing and just acting really annoying. Your parent has to take you aside and talk to you about your attitude—continually. (Remember that word? It means "all the time.") Before you know it, you've missed out on the rides and the shows and the food. All because you chose to have a bad attitude and needed to spend your time being disciplined. That wasn't very smart, was it?

It makes sense to replace complaining with thanksgiving. Start by remembering that nothing you have comes from you. The birthday money you just spent came from God. The athletic or musical skills you have came from God. The house you live in and the car you ride in came from God. Your friends and family came from God. Even the air you breathe comes from God. He is the source of all good things. So do yourself a favor and thank Him continually and in everything.

Write down things you can thank God for today.

_____

_____

_____

Now, write down how you feel after making your thankfulness list. Compare this to how you felt after making your complaining list.

_____

_____

_____

In or For

People sometimes confuse giving thanks *in* everything with giving thanks *for* everything. *In* and *for* are both tiny words, but there is a big difference between them when it comes to giving thanks.

You might be going through a really hard time right now. Maybe your best friend moved away or a family member is ill or kids are not treating you very nicely at school. If it seems impossible to be thankful *for* those things, that's because it is! The good news is that God doesn't expect you to be thankful *for* those things—just *in* those things. And there's a big difference.

God understands that our feelings are real—including fear, anxiety, hurt, and sadness. He wants to help us through the times we're feeling these things, and one of the ways He does that is by encouraging us to remain thankful. The Bible says that we are to give thanks *in* everything because we know that God can and will use it for good when we are called according to His purpose (Romans 8:28). You don't have to thank Him *for* the bully at school or *for* your dad's illness, but you can thank Him when you're *in* that situation. Why? Because thanking God shows that you trust Him to be with you and comfort you and bring you through the difficult time. You're basically thanking Him for being God, which is a really big thing!

What are some things you can thank God *for*?

_____

_____

_____

What are some situations you can thank God *in*?

_____

_____

_____

Now, listen closely here. You need to understand this part. Please keep in mind that you can never say thanks *for* some situations in life because that wouldn't make sense. If something is not good, we shouldn't just pretend that it is. And we shouldn't think it came from God. Sickness doesn't come from God. Bullying doesn't come from God. Sadness doesn't come from God.

Yet whatever situation you find yourself in, you can give thanks *in* it because as a believer in Jesus Christ, you know that God is with you in every situation. And He can use everything—even bad things—for good.

God's Purpose

It's hard to imagine, but pain always has a purpose. When you hurt yourself, you feel the pain because your body needs to let your brain know, "Hey, something happened! You're hurt! Stop and get some help and start the healing process!" After your body has healed, you're good to go.

You may have heard about athletes who have come back from an injury and are better than ever because after the recovery process, they were even more motivated and determined about their training. They worked harder than ever and pushed themselves to new limits. They had a new appreciation for what their bodies could do, and they were excited to see what they could accomplish. That's exactly what God wants you to do when you're feeling pain—and He's right there as your personal trainer, helping you reach new heights.

God has a way of turning a mess into a miracle when we approach that mess with the right heart attitude. If you find yourself in a hard situation—like being the target of bullying—He is there to help you. For example, He will direct you to others who can put a stop to the bullying. And although nobody should be bullied, God can do amazing things through this hard situation. Maybe the bully will have a heart change and come to know Christ. Maybe you will gain the strength to stand up for yourself and others. Maybe the entire culture at your school will change, and everyone will come together to put an end to bullying. When God is involved, nothing is impossible!

What situation in your life seems impossible right now? Write down a prayer asking God to bring something good out of this situation.

_____

_____

_____

God can use *all* things for your good when you love Him and walk in His purpose. God is always creating good things in your life, and even though life doesn't always make sense, He will use every circumstance for your good when you let Him. He can take nothing and make something out of it.

There's a purpose for everything, and when we talk to God and ask Him for guidance, we will find that purpose.

Used by God

Does your family recycle? Do you have a recycling bin at your school? Have you noticed the various recycling containers at places like the grocery store? Many of our communities are getting better and better about recycling. Instead of throwing cans and bottles and papers in the trash, we put them in recycling bins so they can be reused and made into new things.

God is kind of like the ultimate recycler. He can reuse *everything*. All our problems will be used by God. All our pain will be used by God. All our disappointments will be used by God. That fight with your mom? God can use that. The loneliness you feel when you don't have anyone to eat lunch with? God can use that. The fact that your family can't afford to send you to summer camp this year? God can use that.

The fight with your mom might result in you sharing some important stuff with each other. After you fight, you pray and ask God to help you understand each other. And then you talk about the problems and reach some sort of agreement. The next time you're tempted to argue or get mad, you remember that important talk, and you find a better way to solve the problem.

Eating lunch alone can be really tough. Thirty minutes can seem like thirty years when you have nobody to laugh with or talk to. But you can ask God to use that situation for His good, and pretty soon He will show you another person who eats lunch alone. You may realize you have a ton in common, and soon you've found a great new friend—and the two of you invite a few more lonely people to join you at lunch. Suddenly you're part of a super group of friends—a group that includes others because you all know how it feels to be alone.

It may seem like everyone else is going to summer camp and you're the only one who's going to miss out on all the swimming and boating and campfires and horseback riding. You know your family can't afford the cost of camp this year, but you're still sad. But then an opportunity comes along to spend the entire summer working with horses—your absolute favorite thing—at some stables nearby. You don't have to pay a thing, you get to ride horses for free *every day*, and you make some awesome new friends.

See how God can always use a situation for your good? It's okay to feel disappointed or hurt or sad, but always turn to God and ask Him, "Hey, will You show me the good in this? Will You open my eyes to what You're trying to teach me and what You're trying to show me? Will You help me change my attitude and be positive about this whole thing?"

God is greater than any situation, and when we use our words to thank Him *in* everything, we will learn to trust Him more. We can trust Him to turn around any situation and to do good things.

Think about a recent disappointment in your life. What happened? How did God use it for good? (If you haven't seen the good yet, start praying that He will show it to you. He will, and you can come back later and write it down here!)

_____

_____

_____

Trust God

The best way to see the good in things is to trust in God. And we demonstrate our trust in Him by using our words to thank Him *for* lots of things and *In everything*. Remember, you can be thankful to Him *in* something even though you aren't thankful *for* it.

No matter what is wrong in your life, there is always something for which to give thanks. You may never be thankful for the spinach in a smoothie, but you can be thankful for the strawberries and the bananas and the peanut butter that help the spinach go down more easily.

You can always find something to thank God for. If you don't have the latest shoes and you're not happy with the shoes you do have, thank God for your feet. (Seriously!) If you don't have the best singing voice, thank God for the voice you do have, which allows you to talk with your friends and laugh with your family. If you don't have your own room, thank God that you have a warm place to sleep on cold nights. If you don't like the fact that you have to wear a school uniform, thank God that you attend a good school with great teachers and friends.

In every situation, rather than complain, give thanks. Look for the good. For every thing that bothers you, write down five things that make you happy. You can even keep a notebook of things you are grateful for and pull out this notebook when you pray to God. Say the items out loud: "Thank You for fresh strawberries. Thank You for my new bike. Thank You that my mom is feeling better. Thank You for my new baby sister. Thank You for giving me the ability to run fast." This really and truly works!

Giving thanks to God also brings you another benefit: You get peace. Philippians 4:6-7 says, "Don't worry about anything, but in everything, through prayer and petition with thanksgiving, let your requests be made known to God. And the peace of God, which surpasses every thought, will guard your hearts and minds in Christ Jesus."

Again, use your words to give thanks to God *for* everything you can and *in* every situation. In return, He will show you amazing things, teach you important lessons, and draw you closer to Him. It won't always be fun. It won't always be easy. But it *will* always be the right thing to do. Use your words to give thanks. You'll never regret it.

Why is it important to remember to give God thanks for all the great stuff in our lives?

_____

_____

_____

What is the difference between thanking God *for* everything and thanking God *in* everything?

_____

_____

_____

Write down a plan for using your words to be thankful (keeping a thankfulness notebook, putting a sticker on your water bottle that reminds you to give thanks, sticking notes on your bathroom mirror...). Remember to be thankful to God and thankful to others!

_____

_____

_____

Don't Hurt Others with Your Words

an you think of a few things that happen every time you go to the doctor for a checkup? You get weighed and measured, and the nurse checks your blood pressure and heart rate. Then, when the doctor comes in, she asks you to open your mouth, stick out your tongue, and say "aah." When she does this, she's not just checking your tongue or your teeth. She's looking carefully in your mouth because your mouth gives her clues about how healthy the rest of your body is. A healthy mouth usually means a healthy body.

In the same way, what's in your mouth—actually, what comes *out* of your mouth—gives a pretty clear glimpse of what's in your heart. The words you speak show the condition of your heart. Good words usually mean a good heart.

It's kind of like a plant or tree that produces fruit. If every cherry or plum from the tree is moldy or diseased, you can assume that something is wrong with the tree. But if every blueberry or raspberry on the plant is sweet and yummy, the plant itself—which is the source of the fruit— must be healthy.

A good tree will produce good fruit, and a bad tree will produce bad fruit. If the fruit of a tree is good, you can assume the tree is also good. If the fruit of the tree is bad, the tree itself is bad. Your heart is like the tree. And your words are like the fruit of that tree.

Your Words = Your Heart

Jesus tells us in the Bible that the fruit of our mouths— our words—reflect what's in our hearts. "The mouth speaks from the overflow of the heart" (Matthew 12:34). If you make mean comments or use swear words or speak words of gossip, your heart is not healthy.

Trying to fix the bad fruit on a tree without doing anything about the tree itself will never work. You can cut out the diseased spots, but that doesn't change anything. The tree is still unhealthy. If you try to fix your mouth without changing your heart, you're not going to solve the problem. You might be nicer for a day or two, but pretty soon the mean comments or the bad words or the gossip are going to return because you haven't changed your heart.

Now, please don't expect that you're going to be perfect. All of us say things we regret. None of us speaks perfectly. We all say things we wish we hadn't said or use a tone we wish we hadn't used—and we've probably gotten in trouble for those things too. Pay careful attention to what's coming out of your mouth because it reflects the state of your heart.

List some "good fruit" that can come out of a person's mouth. Then list some "bad fruit." How do the words that come out of your mouth reflect the condition of your heart?

_____

_____

_____

What's Inside Shows on the Outside

A girl who has anger in her heart often speaks harsh, mean words that hurt people. A boy with jealousy in his heart puts down others or talks about them behind their backs. A girl with a poor self-image makes constant negative remarks about herself. What's inside shows on the outside when we start talking.

But the heart can be full of good things too! A boy with a heart full of joy speaks words that are positive and encouraging. A girl with love in her heart reaches out to others and connects with them through her words. A boy whose heart is filled with God's power never hesitates to talk with courage and say what is right.

What is inside your heart right now? How does this come out in the things you say?

_____

_____

_____

There's a strong connection between the mouth and the heart. Our heart produces our language. You can try faking it, but that won't work for long. People with kindness in their hearts say kind things. People with meanness in their hearts say mean things.

Pay attention to the condition of your heart. Because if you don't, the chances are very good that you will hurt people with your words. And that's not good for anyone—including you.

Getting Your Heart Right

The best way to get your heart healthy and right is by filling it with God's Word. Psalm 19:14 says, "May the words of my mouth and the meditation of my heart be acceptable to You, LORD, my rock and my Redeemer." That's the goal for all of us. We need to make sure our words and our hearts are acceptable to God.

To get the Word of God into your heart, you need to do more than just quickly read a Bible verse or two and call it good. Memorizing verses is terrific, but you need to do even more than that. You need to keep God's Word constantly in your thoughts.

There are some fun ways to do this. You might write some

favorite verses on sticky notes and put them by your bedside table, or attach them to your bathroom mirror or your school notebook. You can also set aside a specific time each day to read the Bible or a devotional book. Even better, have a friend or your mom or dad join you for your reading time. You can enjoy a favorite snack while you dig into God's Word.

And don't forget to pray. Make sure you have specific times to talk to God—when you get up in the morning, on your bike ride to school, in the shower, whatever works for you—and then remind yourself to talk to God at other times throughout the day too. You can even pray about praying! In the morning tell God, *Please help me remember to talk to You throughout my day.* God will help you remember!

What are some ways you can keep the Word of God constantly in your thoughts?

_____

_____

_____

Also, don't forget to listen! Jesus often said, "He who has ears to hear, let him hear" (Matthew 11:15 NASB). He's not talking about just hearing what was spoken. Or about reading it in a book. Or even reading it in your Bible. Jesus is saying we need to hear God's Word in a way that empowers us to take it in, understand it, and live it out every day. That's how you get your heart in the right place. And when your heart is in the right place, what comes out of your mouth will be right too.

All Your Words Matter

God listens to your every word, including the words you mutter under your breath about your teacher, the "joking" put-downs you direct at your siblings, and the little lies that seem to slip out of your mouth. These small slip-ups may seem to be no big deal, but they show the condition of your heart. And even if they seem harmless, they can actually hurt others. Your teacher might not overhear the words, but your classmates do. Your siblings may smile on the outside at your "jokes," but inside they're hurting. And the little lies add up so that eventually nobody believes you even when you're telling the truth.

Pay attention to your words. You don't have to duct-tape your mouth shut (although sometimes that might seem like the best solution!), but you could try keeping your mouth closed just an extra second or two before you speak. Ask yourself, *Are my words going to help someone else or hurt them?* And make sure you know the answer before you speak.

In order to truly watch your mouth, you need to watch your heart. You do that by thinking before you speak and asking God to help you say the right thing.

Words That Bite

You may have bitten someone with your teeth when you were small, but did you know that you can also bite someone with your words? Your words may not leave teeth marks, but they can do a lot of damage. They can hurt someone on the inside, and it can be very hard for that kind of hurt to heal.

We've all blurted out something in a moment of pain, hurt, or anger and then noticed its damaging effect on another person. Maybe your friend got a horrified look on her face after you said something sarcastic to her. Or your brother said, "I can't believe you just said that!" Or your coach rolled his eyes and lifted his hands in disbelief after hearing the negative words that slipped out of your mouth.

You've also probably been on the receiving end of words that bite.

How do you feel when someone attacks you with words that bite? What can you do to avoid speaking damaging words to others?

_____

_____

_____

We hear so many put-downs and sarcastic comments on TV shows and in movies and read so many not-so-nice remarks online that it's easy to forget the effect our negative words have on others. We jokingly call our friend a loser or ugly without understanding that comments like that can really hurt a person. Before you say something, ask yourself how you would feel if that comment were directed at you. If you aren't sure how you would feel (or if you know that it would make you feel bad), don't say it!

Gossip

Do you want to avoid problems with other people? Probably the best advice I can give you for doing this is one thing: Avoid gossip. The Bible says, "The one who reveals secrets is a constant gossip; avoid someone with a big mouth"

(Proverbs 20:19). Avoid people who have a big mouth, and avoid being a person who has a big mouth.

A gossip is a person who tells other people's secrets and talks about people behind their backs and sometimes even makes up stuff that isn't true about other people. Gossips don't care about anyone's privacy. They just care about having the latest dirt to spread. If anyone ever starts a conversation with "I shouldn't be telling you this…" or "I promised not to say anything, but…" stop the conversation right there! You don't have to make a big deal about it. Just say, "Hey, I don't really need to hear this. Let's talk about something else." And then change the subject. Right away.

Instead of being a gossip or listening to a gossip, hang out with trustworthy people—and be trustworthy yourself. Someone who doesn't spread rumors. Someone who knows when to keep quiet. Someone who can be depended on to be there for a friend.

God's heart hurts when He hears us hurting each other. He loves us so much that He sent His Son to die for us, and He has determined that every one of us is worthy of His love and care. We sometimes forget that we make God sad when we say mean words or gossip about someone else. We forget that the Lord loves this person as much as He loves us, and hurting them with our words hurts God too.

Now, one word of caution. Sometimes a person might tell you information that you need to pass on to a responsible adult. For example, if a friend threatens to hurt himself, you need to tell someone. Keep in mind that a gossip never seeks to help or heal. They just want to be the center of attention and get others to listen to their juicy news reports. If it would hurt the person *not* to share what they told you, you need to tell a parent or teacher or another adult you trust.

How can you tell the difference between gossip and information that should be shared with someone else?

_____

_____

_____

One of the reasons why people gossip, and one reason why you may find yourself gossiping, has to do with having too much time on your hands. If you're bored, you're more likely to gossip. You spend time on social media. You send text messages. Before you know it, you're spreading rumors and information because you're addicted to the responses you get back. Gossip has become a source of entertainment. But people should never be used for entertainment. Find something else to do, and pay attention to how you are using your time and your mouth.

When you're tempted to gossip and talk about other people behind their backs, what are some things you can do instead? It's always good to have a plan for getting rid of gossip!

_____

_____

_____

DON'T HURT EACH OTHER

One time when my brother and I were kids, he did something entirely wrong. Being the self-appointed police in the life of my siblings, I told my dad, and he let my brother have it. My brother got what we called a "session." Yet when my brother's session was done, my dad called me in for mine as well. I was in complete shock and disbelief!

"What?" I asked.

"You heard me. It's your turn," my dad replied.

I asked my dad why, and he responded, "You could have helped your brother realize what he was doing was wrong and helped him stop it on his own. If your motivation had been love for your brother, that's what you would have done. Instead, you just wanted to get him in trouble. So because of that, you're in trouble too."

In a family, the goal is not to hurt each other but rather to help each other become as strong and mature as possible. The same is true in the family of God. As believers, we are supposed to help each other and love each other, not worry about which one of us is the better Christian. God doesn't play favorites. He loves all of us, and all of us are to love and help each other.

Help, Not Harm

God wants us to create an environment that helps others instead of harming them. When we honor God with the words that come out of our mouths, we do our part in creating this environment. Wouldn't you prefer to live in a world where people help each other?

Words are powerful. For good and for bad. And once spoken, they are difficult to retrieve.

How easy is it to squeeze toothpaste out of a tube? Super easy, right? But what if I told you that after you'd squeezed it out, you needed to put it back in the tube. That would be impossible! Just as it is impossible to put toothpaste back in a tube, you can never put words back in your mouth after you've spoken them. They're out, and there's not much you can do to stuff them back in.

You may think getting this good-words thing down is impossible, but God doesn't. He has faith in you! The Bible says, "I am able to do all things through Him who strengthens me" (Philippians 4:13). God is transforming you from the inside out, which means you are able to do great things for Him. So go after it. Ask Him to use your words to accomplish amazing things, and He'll make sure He does just that in your life.

Beware of Lies

Can you remember the first lie you told? Probably not. Even if we don't intend to tell lies, sometimes they just slip out. Maybe we tell a lie to avoid getting in trouble. Or to avoid getting someone else in trouble. Or to make ourselves look better.

People lie for a lot of reasons. To impress people. To trick people. To get revenge. To get something good for themselves. To get back at others. To avoid being punished. And on and on.

But we shouldn't lie. God is a God of truth, and He commands us to be people of truth (1 John 1:5-10). When we lie, we hurt ourselves, and we hurt others. People lose trust in us. The next time we tell them something, they wonder if we're telling the truth.

Remember the two questions you should always ask yourself if you're unsure of what to say: *Is it kind? Is it true?* Make sure the answer to both questions is a definite yes before you let any words escape from your mouth.

What happened the last time you told a lie? How did other people respond to you? What two questions can you ask yourself next time you're tempted to say something that might be a lie?

MOUTHWASH

A lot of people need mouthwash in the morning. It helps us get rid of the germs and bacteria that collected overnight. In fact, many of us could stand to use mouthwash after lunch and dinner as well.

That's why breath mints and gum are so popular. All these successful products have become normal and natural parts of our lives simply because fighting nasty breath has become a normal and natural part of our lives. Mouthwash, breath mints, and chewing gum are designed to cleanse the mouth from the things that cause bad breath. They attack the source of bad breath so people won't mind being around us when we speak to them.

When you stop to pay attention to your words and make sure that God will be pleased with what you say, you're basically using spiritual mouthwash. You won't make people back away from you because what comes out of your mouth stinks. Instead, people will want to be around you. So keep using that spiritual mouthwash. It's proven to work!

Bad Words

Between television and movies, social media and the internet, bad language seems to be no big deal in our world today. But it *is* a big deal. Like everything else that comes out of your mouth, bad words show that there are bad thoughts and negative ideas in your heart.

Be honest. What is your heart-level reaction when you hear someone swearing? I hope you don't think they're cool or that you want to be like them. I hope you realize that the bad attitude of their heart is coming out in their words—words that God tells us we shouldn't speak because they do nothing to help build others up.

In Ephesians 4:29 we read, "No foul language is to come from your mouth, but only what is good for building up someone in need, so that it gives grace to those who hear." Christians who are serious about their faith and following Jesus should not be known for the bad words coming from their mouths.

You can't help what you hear all around you. You can't control what other people are saying. But you *can* control your own mouth. You may not be able to stop other people from using bad words around you, but you can stop yourself from joining in.

And yet sometimes you *can* make a difference. All it takes is for one or two people to agree not to use swear words, and the language of an entire group can change. Someone probably notices that you and your friend don't swear, and that makes them notice it more when they *do* swear. Without really thinking about it, they swear less. And that has an effect on the whole group.

When you find yourself tempted to talk like other kids so that you fit in, remember that it's really important to God that you follow Him and do what He wants you to do. Remind yourself that you are called to be *in* the world but not *of* the world (John 17:15-16). When it comes to your mouth, God expects His followers to have a higher standard than the world does.

When you feel like you want to talk like other kids and fit in, what can you do? What does God want you to do?

_____

_____

_____

Taking the Lord's Name in Vain

We also need to talk about the ways in which we use God's name. He doesn't want His name to be used as an exclamation point (Matthew 5:33-37; James 5:12). Rather, He wants His name to be used only when it reflects how amazing and glorious He is (Psalm 29:1-2).

The Bible lists this as one of the Ten Commandments, which God gave Moses when developing His relationship with the nation of Israel and ultimately with us (see Exodus 20:1-17). What does it mean to "take the Lord's name in vain"? The Holman Christian Standard Bible says, "Do not misuse the name of the LORD your God." It means saying God's name in emptiness, without worth, purpose, or value. We do this when we say God's name as a cuss word. We also say this when we attach swear words to God's name. Or even just when we use His name as an exclamation.

Just don't go there. Ever. Decide to be someone who doesn't use God's name in a negative way. After all, how would you feel if you heard your own name put down, tossed under the bus, or dismissed? Why would God feel any less strongly about His own name? And yet people do that all the time to the God who created them, gives them life, and loves them enough to send His only Son to die for their sins. God is holy, and His name is holy. We need to honor that.

Watch Your Words

We limit the work God can do in our lives when we constantly use bad and negative words. That's because our words reflect what's in our hearts, and a heart that is filled with God's love and truth has no space for anything that is harmful or negative.

If you want to use your words to help others and to make the world a happier, more positive place, keep God close. Read the Bible. Pray. Constantly be asking God to help you learn and grow and become more like Him.

Remember that your words include more than the words you say out loud. They include what you text or write. They even include pictures you post. Anything that sends a message. They even include the words you just think about yourself and about others.

Dealing with your tongue may be hard. Your words won't always be perfect. You'll say things you wish you could take back. You'll mess up and speak words that aren't kind. You'll slip and let things that aren't truthful escape from your mouth. But keep trying. You've got this! God is there to help you every step of the way.

Don't be afraid to ask someone else for help too. Tell a friend or a family member or a church leader what you're trying to do. Say, "Hey, I'm really trying to watch my words. I want the things that come out of my mouth to be pleasing to God. I'm tired of hurting people and wishing I could take back what I said. Can you call me on anything you hear me say that I shouldn't? I promise I won't get mad. I really need help here!"

Our words are powerful—and we should never take them lightly. Your words affect not only those who are listening to you but also yourself. Make it your goal to use your mouth wisely and watch God move in your life in ways you never could have dreamed. Turn your heart toward God, and your words will follow.

Good words come from a good heart. Make a decision to be someone who helps others rather than hurting them, and let your words show what God is doing in your heart.

REFLECTION: YOUR WORD AND GOD'S WORD

How do the words that come out of your mouth show what is in your heart? If you need to change your words, what do you need to work on first?

_____

_____

_____

What are some types of talk that we should avoid? Write down a prayer asking God to help you avoid these types of talk.

_____

_____

_____

What kind of words hurt others? What kind of words help others? What kind of person do you want to be—a helping person or a hurting person? How can God help you be the kind of person you want to be?

_____

_____

_____

PS

We've covered a lot of ground here! But before you head out into the world, let's talk a little bit more about the importance of words in your life. You're at an age where the way you talk will help determine the direction you go in life. That's because your words come from your heart, and what's in your heart shows the kind of person you are right now as well as the kind of person you're going to become.

The older you get, the more life choices you are able to make. When you were a baby, pretty much all your choices were made for you. Sure, nobody could force you to eat or sleep, but you didn't really have a choice in most things. What you wore, where you went, and even what you ate and where you slept (and often what time you slept) were all determined for you. Babies *need* someone to do basically everything for them because they're helpless on their own.

As you became older, you got to choose more and more things for yourself. And you also learned more and more words so you could express yourself. I'm sure that as a toddler, you were very familiar with the word "no." And you might have been that independent little kid who liked to say, "I do it myself!"

Now you're doing many things for yourself, including choosing your own words. You're no longer that small child learning what things are named and repeating words after listening to your parents and older siblings say them. When you were first learning words, you didn't notice the effect your speech had on other people. Yes, you may have smiled when people laughed at the cute and funny ways you mispronounced certain words. But you didn't truly have the ability to think about what you were saying and understand the way your words could affect others.

Now, though, your words have power. They have power to make a friend feel better when she's having a bad day. They have power to encourage your brother when he loses his championship baseball game. They have power to make your neighbor smile when you say her garden looks pretty. And best of all, they have power to introduce someone to Jesus, which is life-changing power!

Besides the power to do good things, your words also have power to do bad things. They have power to make your friend feel sad when you tease him. They have power to hurt your mom when you yell at her and talk back to her. They have power to tear down your classmates' self-esteem when you say mean things to them or gossip about them. Negative words have life-changing power too.

Get into the habit of thinking about the words you use.

Words are life-changing, after all. Ask God to help guide your speech. Learn to think of others before you think of yourself, which includes thinking about the effect your words have on other people. Tell God, *Please help me think about the things I say. Make me aware of the times I tell a lie or gossip or make a comment I shouldn't make. And please help me notice how my words affect others.*

And while you're considering your words, also consider the many ways in which you use words. Sure, you use them when you're having a face-to-face conversation with another person. You also use them when you're texting on your phone. Or making comments on social media sites. Or even thinking them to yourself.

There's one more thing I'd like you to think about. When you were little, you learned words by hearing them. Other people spoke words, and you imitated what they said. You can hear the beginnings of this in a tiny baby's babbles and coos. That type of learning continues all through life. The more you hear of something, the more you tend to imitate it.

If you hang out with people who say negative things, you're going to be more likely to say negative things. If your friends like to gossip, you'll get caught up in that. If the kids you spend time with use swear words or say mean things, you'll probably find yourself doing the same thing. It's hard to be surrounded by people who act a certain way and not start acting that way yourself.

The good news is that the opposite is true. If you hang out with people who say positive things, you're going to be more likely to say positive things. If you hang out with people who are truthful, it will be natural for you to be truthful. If you spend time with kids who are kind, you'll find it much easier to be kind. If your friends are happy and encouraging, you will take on those traits and be happy and encouraging.

Lastly, don't forget to hang out with God! The best words of all are found in His Word, the Bible. Spend time reading the words He has to say. Memorize verses that tell you how you're supposed to speak. (You can highlight all the verses used in this book. That will give you a great start!) Pay attention to the words spoken at church by your pastor or your Sunday school teacher or your youth group leader. Those people are getting direction from God, and their words are inspired by Him. And listen for God speaking to you personally. You talk to Him, but He also talks to you!

Your words matter. Your words have power. If your heart is in the right place—if you're walking with Jesus and focused on others and doing your best to live a life that's pleasing to God—you will be speaking the right kind of words. There's nothing more powerful than that!

Now get out there and change your world by using the best words you can!

A Kid's Guide to the Names of God

You can build your self-confidence and understand who you are in Christ by learning the names of God. You'll also discover how God's names reveal His characteristics, which can help you overcome whatever challenge you face in life.

A Kid's Guide to the Armor of God

If you're between the ages of eight and twelve, you'll enjoy this helpful guide to the armor of God. Pastor and author Tony Evans shows you how to dress in the armor God provides so you'll able to speak the truth, stand firm in the faith, and spread the good news of Jesus.

The Awesome Book of Bible Answers for Kids

You probably have lots of important questions about Jesus, God, and faith. Respected Christian teacher Josh McDowell answers your questions straight from the Bible—in language that's easy to understand.

Bible Basics for Kids

In this fun, easy-to-read exploration of God, the Bible, and faith, kids like you can discover speedy summaries of *every* book of Scripture, a 90-day reading plan, memorization tricks, and more. Terry Glaspey and Kathleen Kerr make clear that the Bible is all about God reaching out to His children through Jesus.

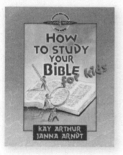

How to Study Your Bible for Kids

One of America's best-loved Bible teachers shows kids like you how to study the Bible yourself in three steps—observation, interpretation, and application. You'll discover that God's Word still applies today, and you'll better understand God's love for you.

To learn more about Harvest House books and
to read sample chapters, visit our website:

www.harvesthousepublishers.com

HARVEST HOUSE PUBLISHERS
EUGENE, OREGON